DATE DUE

JUL 0 6 2012		
JUN 1 7 2013		
MAR 1 1 2014		

EDGE BOOKS

EQUIPPED FOR BATTLE

WEAPONS, GEAR, AND UNIFORMS

❖ OF ❖

WORLD WAR II

by Michael Burgan

Consultant:
Jennifer L. Jones
Chair, Armed Forces History
NMAH, Smithsonian Institution
Washington, D.C.

CAPSTONE PRESS
a capstone

Edge Books are published by Capstone Press,
1710 Roe Crest Drive, North Mankato, Minnesota 56003.
www.capstonepub.com

Library of Congress Cataloging-in-Publication Data
Burgan, Michael.
    Weapons, gear, and uniforms of World War II / by Michael Burgan.
    p. cm.—(Edge books)
    Includes bibliographical references and index.
    Audience: Grades 4-6.
    Summary: "Describes the uniforms, gear, and weapons used by the Axis Powers and
Allied Powers during World War II"—Provided by publisher.
    ISBN 978-1-4296-7650-2 (library binding)
    1. World War, 1939–1945—Equipment and supplies—Juvenile literature. 2. Military
weapons—History—20th century—Juvenile literature. I. Title. II. Series.
D743.7.B87 2012
940.54'83—dc23   2011028687

Editorial Credits

Aaron Sautter, editor; Ted Williams, designer; Eric Manske, production specialist

Photo Credits

AP Images, 10 (top); Corbis, 11 (both), 12 (top), Hulton-Deutsch Collection, 10 (bottom);
Corel, 17 (bottom); Gamma-Keystone via Getty Images/Keystone-France, 9 (top); Getty
Images: AFP/STF, 4, Archive Photos, 26 (top), Dorling Kindersley/Gary Ombler, 12 (bottom),
13 (top), Hulton Archive, 27 (bottom), Hulton Archive/FPG, 19 (top), Hulton Archive/
Galerie Bilderwelt, 9 (bottom), 23 (bottom), Hulton Archive/Keystone, 27 (top), 28 (left),
Michael Ochs Archives, 21 (bottom), Popperfoto, 8, 19 (bottom), Roger Viollet, 24 (bottom),
26 (bottom), Time Life Pictures/Charles E. Steinheimer, cover (soldiers), Time Life Pictures/
David E. Scherman, 20 (bottom), Time Life Pictures/Mansell, 22, Time Life Pictures/Margaret
Bourke-White, 13 (bottom), Time Life Pictures/US Air Force, cover (aircraft); James P.
Rowan, 18 (bottom), 24 (top), 25 (top); NARA, 29 (bottom); Newscom: akg-images, 23 (top),
Photoshot/War/UPPA, 28 (right); Shutterstock: Adrian Grosu, 18 (top), Gary Blakelev, 14
(bottom), Michaela Stejskalova, 15 (top), Olemac, 14 (top), 15 (bottom), 18 (middle), Sergey
Kamshylin, cover (cannon); Wikimedia, 21 (top), Antique Military Rifles, 16 (bottom),
Dkamm, 16 (top), German Federal Archive/Esselborn, 25 (bottom), German Federal Archive/
Toni Schneiders, 20 (top), USAF photo, 29 (top), USMC photo, 17 (top)

Artistic Effects

iStockphoto: Duncan Walker; Shutterstock: Eky Studio, Ewa Walicka,
hektor2, maigi

Printed in the United States of America in Stevens Point, Wisconsin.
102011   006404WZS12

TABLE OF CONTENTS

On September 1, 1939, German forces invaded Poland. It was the first military action of World War II (1939–1945). Taking over Poland was the first part of German leader Adolf Hitler's plan to control Europe. Italy later joined Germany to fight in Europe. Japan allied itself with Germany and fought in Asia and the Pacific. Together, the three major nations were known as the Axis powers.

Opposing them was a **coalition** of dozens of countries known as the Allies. The major Allied nations included Great Britain, France, the Soviet Union, and China. The United States joined the Allies in 1941. The Allies fought to defend themselves and to stop the Axis powers from taking over other nations.

World War II was the deadliest conflict the world has ever seen. Major battles raged across five continents and several oceans. By the time the war ended in 1945, more than 70 million people were dead. Millions more were homeless and starving. Never before had the world seen death and destruction on such a huge scale.

coalition—an alliance of people, groups, or countries working toward a common goal

Several new weapons were developed during World War II. Many of them had the most advanced features of the time. Improved versions of tanks, rockets, and machine guns began to appear on the battlefield. But soldiers still used reliable older weapons and gear to survive in combat.

WORLD WAR II CASUALTIES

NATION	TOTAL MILITARY CASUALTIES
China	3,500,000
France	250,000
Germany	11,500,000
Great Britain	1,055,000
Italy	600,000
Japan	2,100,000
Soviet Union	23,600,000
United States	1,099,000

* Casualties include soldiers who were killed, wounded, or missing in action.

BATTLE FACT

On December 7, 1941, Japan launched a surprise attack on the U.S. naval base at Pearl Harbor, Hawaii. The attack brought the United States into World War II. More than 2,300 U.S. soldiers and sailors died at Pearl Harbor that day.

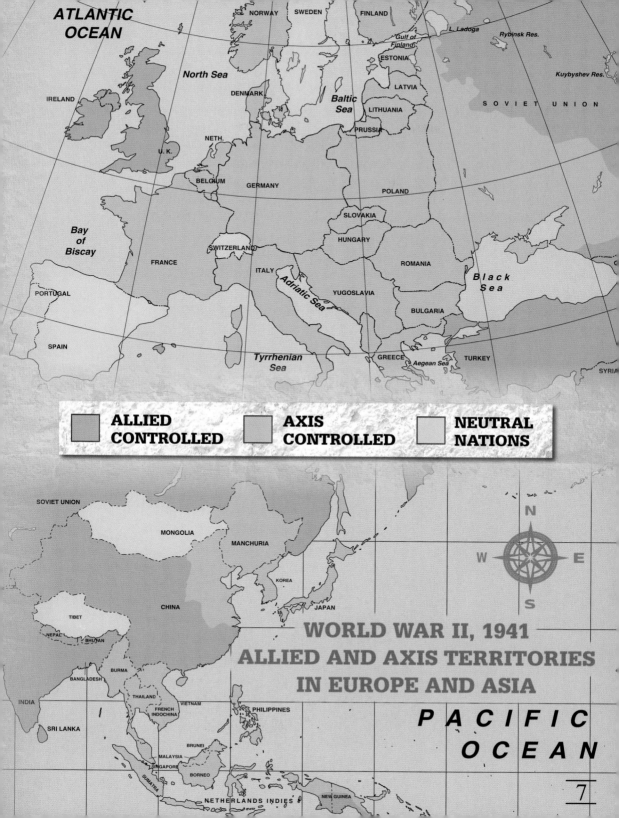

ATLANTIC OCEAN

NORWAY SWEDEN FINLAND

North Sea

Gulf of Finland
L. Ladoga
Rybinsk Res.

ESTONIA

Kuybyshev Res.

IRELAND

DENMARK

Baltic Sea

LATVIA

LITHUANIA

S O V I E T   U N I O N

NETH.

U.K.

BELGIUM

GERMANY

PRUSSIA

POLAND

Bay of Biscay

SWITZERLAND

FRANCE

SLOVAKIA

HUNGARY

ROMANIA

ITALY

Adriatic Sea

YUGOSLAVIA

Black Sea

PORTUGAL

BULGARIA

SPAIN

Tyrrhenian Sea

GREECE

Aegean Sea

TURKEY

SYRIA

ALLIED CONTROLLED	AXIS CONTROLLED	NEUTRAL NATIONS

SOVIET UNION

MONGOLIA

MANCHURIA

KOREA

CHINA

JAPAN

TIBET

NEPAL

BHUTAN

BURMA

BANGLADESH

INDIA

THAILAND

FRENCH INDOCHINA

VIETNAM

PHILIPPINES

SRI LANKA

BRUNEI

MALAYSIA

SINGAPORE

BORNEO

SUMATRA

NETHERLANDS INDIES

NEW GUINEA

WORLD WAR II, 1941
ALLIED AND AXIS TERRITORIES
IN EUROPE AND ASIA

PACIFIC OCEAN

N

W   E

S

Uniforms on both sides varied depending on a soldier's specific rank and job. Clothes made with certain color patterns called camouflage were common. Camouflage made it harder for enemies to see soldiers. Men doing construction work or maintaining machinery commonly wore casual clothing. They often got dirty and needed simple, cheap uniforms.

U.S. HELMETS

For a U.S. **infantry** soldier, the most important part of the uniform was a metal helmet. Helmets came in different shapes, but all offered protection from enemy fire.

U.S. INFANTRY UNIFORMS

The typical U.S. soldier wore olive-colored pants and shirts. Canvas leggings covered the bottom part of the pants. As the war went on, most soldiers switched to high boots made of leather.

infantry—a group of soldiers trained to fight and travel on foot

GERMAN INFANTRY UNIFORMS

German infantry troops typically wore gray-green uniforms. Uniform shirts, called field tunics, had four front pockets. When not in battle, the soldiers wore basic field caps.

OFFICERS' INSIGNIA

Officers from both sides wore **insignia** to show their rank. German naval captains had four gold bars and a gold star on their shirt cuffs. U.S. officers wore a variety of stripes and bars on their sleeves. High ranking U.S. officers like colonels and generals wore silver bars, eagles, or stars on their collars.

WOMEN'S DRESS UNIFORMS

During the war, several million women joined their country's military or found ways to help in the war effort. Women's formal uniforms usually included dresses or skirts.

insignia—a badge or design that shows someone's rank or membership in an organization

SPECIALIZED UNIFORMS

Many troops faced extreme weather conditions. They fought in steamy jungles, freezing mountains, and hot deserts. Different climates forced both the Axis and Allied militaries to create specialized uniforms. Soldiers had to be protected from the weather and still be able to fight on the battlefield.

COOL CLOTHING

African deserts and Asian jungles could be very hot. Soldiers in these locations often wore shorts to beat the heat. Desert clothes were usually a light brown color to match the desert sands. Some soldiers also wore sun helmets with a wide brim that offered extra protection from the sun.

WADING SUITS

Some Soviet soldiers wore a special wading uniform. The suit helped soldiers cross rivers. It had rubber overalls that covered most of the body. The soldiers also wore an inflatable rubber tube around their waist.

LEATHER PILOT SUITS

Airplanes were unheated, so warm clothing was important for pilots. Pilots often wore leather clothing lined with a type of wool called fleece. Some pilots wore specialized suits that were heated by electricity.

FROGMEN

U.S. Navy divers called frogmen often wore simple swimsuits on their missions. The divers were nicknamed "naked warriors." Frogmen also wore large rubber flippers and plastic masks to help them move easily underwater.

WINTER COATS

Soldiers in cold winter climates often wore thick coats with hoods. The coats helped the men stay warm, but they often could not move easily on the battlefield. Winter clothing was sometimes white to blend in with the snow.

SPECIALIZED EQUIPMENT

Military forces in World War II needed many kinds of specialized gear to do their jobs. Officers used radios to communicate with soldiers on the battlefield. Troops injured in battle needed first-aid care. And some specialized equipment helped troops avoid deadly situations in the first place.

MINE DETECTORS

Both Axis and Allied forces buried **land mines** to blow up passing vehicles and troops. Some soldiers used mine detectors to locate these deadly devices. The first electronic mine detector was invented during the war. It used magnets and made a noise when it detected metal underground.

MEDICAL KITS

Medics were trained to treat serious battlefield injuries. Their kits contained bandages, medicine, medical knives, and tools to remove bullets. Most soldiers also carried smaller first-aid kits.

land mine—an explosive triggered by weight; land mines are usually hidden just under the surface of the ground

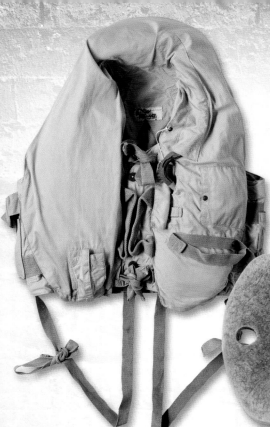

LIFE JACKETS

Life jackets were an important piece of safety equipment for sailors and pilots. The jackets kept the men floating if they ended up in the water. Some jackets were made with lightweight materials that floated easily. Other jackets filled with air when a cord was pulled.

BATTLE FACT

Spies on both sides used a variety of special tools. Spies could hide knives inside their shoes. Tiny cameras could be hidden inside matchboxes. Small, thin knives could fit inside pencils. These tools helped spies carry out dangerous missions deep in enemy territory.

FIELD RADIOS

Radio operators carried portable, battery-powered radios. One common U.S. model fit into a backpack. Radios greatly increased a commander's ability to direct his troops on the battlefield. Some radios sent their signals over wires. Soldiers carried rolls of radio wire onto the battlefield to connect commanders with their troops.

AXIS POWERS LIGHT GUNS AND BLADES

Axis soldiers used several different rifles, pistols, and bladed weapons. Soldiers sometimes fought with knives in hand-to-hand combat. Officers wore swords, but they were used mainly for ceremonies. Machine guns could fire hundreds of rounds of ammunition in only a few seconds.

MAUSER RIFLES

The German army commonly used Mauser rifles. Mauser clips typically held five bullets. After firing, the shooter slid a metal bar called a bolt to push a new bullet into the gun's chamber.

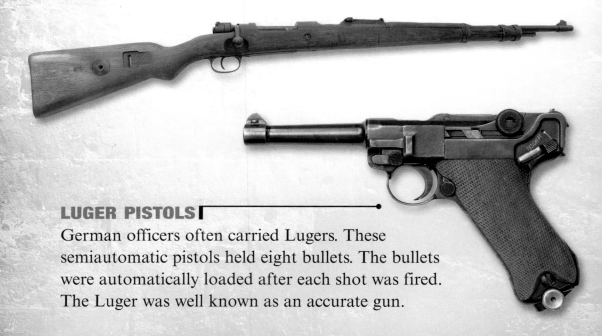

LUGER PISTOLS

German officers often carried Lugers. These semiautomatic pistols held eight bullets. The bullets were automatically loaded after each shot was fired. The Luger was well known as an accurate gun.

✤ **ammunition**—bullets and other objects fired from weapons

MP40 SUBMACHINE GUNS

A submachine gun uses gases created inside the gun. The gases move a spring that ejects used casings and loads fresh bullets. Machine guns could be easily carried and fired by one person. The German MP40 was designed for close combat. It could fire at a rate of 500 rounds per minute.

ARISAKA TYPE 38 CARBINES

Some soldiers used shorter bolt-action carbines. A soldier had to move the gun's bolt to load a bullet manually. The shorter barrel made it easier to carry. Japanese **paratroopers** often used the Arisaka Type 38 carbine.

TACHI SWORDS

Japanese officers carried a variety of swords, including the tachi. These swords were usually worn to honor the skills of ancient samurai warriors. But some officers were trained to use them in combat.

paratrooper—a soldier who is trained to jump by parachute into battle

ALLIED POWERS LIGHT GUNS AND BLADES

Like the Axis powers, the Allies fought with a variety of handheld weapons such as bolt-action rifles and submachine guns. Some special forces carried out missions behind enemy lines. To avoid raising an alarm, they carried special knives that could take out enemies quickly and quietly.

COLT .45 PISTOLS

Most U.S. troops carried the Colt .45 semiautomatic pistol as a sidearm. It fired slightly larger bullets than the revolvers it replaced. This gun is still made today.

MOSIN-NAGANT M1891 SNIPER RIFLES

Snipers used powerful rifles such as the Soviet-made Mosin-Nagant. These guns allowed snipers to hide in a protected location and fire accurately on enemies from a distance. The Soviets made more than 300,000 of these rifles. Some came with telescopes that helped snipers shoot even more accurately.

BATTLE FACT
With a telescope, Mosin-Nagant rifles were accurate up to about 2,400 feet (732 meters).

BROWNING AUTOMATIC RIFLES (BARS)

The Allies had machine guns of all sizes. One light machine gun was the Browning automatic rifle. It could fire at a rate of 500 rounds per minute. The rapid fire of a machine gun makes the barrel very hot. Some World War II machine guns used a water system to keep the barrel cool. But the Browning relied on air to stay cool.

STEN SUBMACHINE GUNS

British troops often used Sten submachine guns. The guns cost only about $10 to make. They were easy to use, but many soldiers didn't like them because they tended to be unreliable in combat.

COMBAT KNIVES

Both British and U.S. forces used "knuckleduster" knives. The handle had metal rings that fit around the fingers. If the soldier couldn't use the blade, he could still punch enemies with the metal rings. Another common combat knife was the Fairbairn-Sykes knife. This British knife had a deadly double-edged blade.

EXPLOSIVES AND SPECIALIZED WEAPONS

Millions of explosive devices were used during the war. Soldiers often carried hand grenades into battle. Land mines and sea mines were easily hidden to take out enemy troops and ships. Certain specialized weapons appeared for the first time during the war.

U.S. "PINEAPPLE" GRENADES

U.S. soldiers often used "pineapple" grenades, which got their nickname from the fruit they resemble. The thrower first pulled out a pin that kept a lever in place. Releasing the lever set off a four-second fuse. The grenade blew up four seconds after a soldier threw it.

GERMAN STICK GRENADES

German stick grenades were primed to explode by pulling a cord inside the wooden handle. The thrower had about four seconds to safely throw it at the enemy.

LAND MINES

These small explosives were buried underground. Some were designed to explode when enemy troops stepped on them. Larger land mines could take out tanks and other heavy vehicles.

FLAMETHROWERS

Flamethrowers were useful in driving enemy forces out of well-protected hiding places. The typical flamethrower used two tanks. One held fuel that was lit by a small flame at the end of the barrel. The other tank held a gas that forced the fuel out of the barrel. Both Axis and Allied forces used flamethrowers in the war.

BAZOOKAS

The U.S. military developed bazookas during the war. These weapons were light enough for one soldier to fire. The shells they launched were powerful enough to destroy a tank.

BATTLE FACT

About 300 million anti-tank mines were used during World War II. Countries are still discovering old, unexploded mines more than 70 years after the war ended.

MISSILES AND SMART BOMBS

In addition to small, handheld weapons, both sides used powerful artillery weapons. Field artillery sat on wheeled carriages and were towed by jeeps or trucks. Larger units were armored and could be driven like tanks. Howitzers and mortars were designed to fire over long distances or over tall objects.

SMALL ARTILLERY

Several countries developed small artillery. The German LG40 could be separated into several pieces and dropped by parachute from planes. Soldiers could use the powerful gun to launch surprise attacks behind enemy lines.

HOWITZERS

Howitzers were common in the war. These artillery units needed several men to load, aim, and fire their heavy shells. One large U.S. howitzer, nicknamed "Long Tom," could hit targets up to 13 miles (21 kilometers) away.

KARL-GERÄT HOWITZERS

Germany created the largest of the self-propelled howitzers. The *Karl-Gerät* could fire a **projectile** that weighed nearly 5,000 pounds (2,268 kilograms).

NAVAL ARTILLERY

Battleships carried the largest naval guns. The guns sat in movable housings called turrets. Turrets could easily turn to fire at moving targets. They also protected the gun crew inside.

M1 MORTARS

The U.S.-made M1 mortar required a team of three to carry it and set it up. The M1 was sometimes used to fire smoke bombs that made it hard for enemy troops to see the battlefield.

 projectile—an object that is thrown or shot through the air

SPECIALIZED HEAVY GUNS

Some heavy artillery pieces were designed for special tasks. Anti-aircraft (AA) guns were designed to accurately fire shells at enemy planes up to 7 miles (11 km) high. Anti-tank guns fired shells strong enough to pierce a tank's armor. Other heavy guns included cannons that sat on railroad cars and fired giant shells at targets miles away.

BRITISH MK III ANTI-AIRCRAFT GUNS

Powerful British 3.7-inch (9.4-cm) MK III guns fired 28-pound (13-kg) shells. They could hit targets up to 6 miles (9.7 km) high. Sometimes gunners used radar to help aim the gun.

 radar—a device that uses radio waves to track the location of objects

GERMAN RAILWAY GUNS

During World War I (1914–1918), several armies used large artillery that had to be moved on railroad cars. Some of these were also used in World War II. Germany built most of these large guns. The K5 "Leopold" could fire a shell almost 39 miles (63 km).

BATTLE FACT

The largest railway gun of the war was nicknamed "Gustav." It could fire a 7-ton (6.4-metric ton) projectile up to 24 miles (39 km) away. It took hundreds of men and three weeks to assemble the German gun.

FLAK 88 ANTI-TANK GUN

With its wheels off, this German gun sat low to the ground. The Flak 88 was a semiautomatic gun. Its shells could pierce armor more than 6 inches (15 cm) thick.

BOFORS GUNS

Bofors anti-aircraft guns were used on land and at sea. The Swedish-built weapons could fire rapidly. However, their shells could only reach targets flying less than 1.4 miles (2.2 km) high.

TANKS

Tanks played a major role in battles across Europe. By using tracks instead of wheels, they could move easily off roads. Some armies took the basic tank frame and used it as the base for powerful tank destroyers. Some nations also relied on half-tracks, which had both tracks and wheels.

SHERMAN M4 TANKS

Sherman tanks weren't the most powerful, but U.S. factories built huge numbers of them. About 40,000 Shermans were built during the war. In addition to the main gun, Shermans carried several machine guns.

M3 HALF-TRACKS

Half-tracks were used to carry troops, anti-aircraft guns, and artillery. The vehicles were used by many Allied nations. They could move easily over wet ground and snow.

SOVIET T-34S

Military experts consider the T-34 one of the best tanks ever made. The Soviet-built tank combined speed, thick armor, and great firepower. These tanks were also easy to build, so they could be quickly replaced if destroyed in battle.

FUNNIES

The British made several specialized tanks. They were often called "funnies" because of their various designs. They included flame-throwing tanks, mine-sweeping tanks, and bulldozer-style tanks.

PANZER IV "TIGERS"

The German Tiger had an 88 mm gun. It was one of the largest guns on any tank of the war. The Tiger's thick armor helped protect it from enemy shells.

PLANES AND SHIPS

Airplanes were among the most important weapons used in the war. Bombers and fighters carried out countless missions. Meanwhile, ships also played a key role in many nations' war efforts. They carried troops, fired at land targets, launched aircraft, and battled other ships.

B-24 LIBERATORS

The B-24 Liberator flew missions everywhere the Allies fought. The U.S. bomber carried a crew of 10 and could fly a round trip of 3,000 miles (4,828 km). The plane also carried 10 machine guns to defend itself from enemy planes.

JAPANESE ZERO FIGHTER PLANES

Japanese Zero planes were some of the best fighters over the Pacific Ocean. The planes had a top speed of 310 miles (499 km) per hour. They were much faster than the U.S. fighters they faced.

LANDING CRAFT, MECHANIZED (LCM)

Landing craft, like the American-made LCM, were designed for **amphibious attacks**. They carried troops and equipment from large ships to shore.

AIRCRAFT CARRIERS

Aircraft carriers became the most important ships in naval fleets. With about 100 planes, carriers were like floating airfields. Each ship had a control center called an island on the top deck. Crews controlled takeoffs and landings of planes from the ship's island.

GERMAN U-BOATS

German submarines were known as U-boats, which stood for "undersea boats." U-boats carried a crew of 24 men. They were used to target the Allies' supply ships in the North Atlantic.

 amphibious attack—a military action involving forces landing and attacking from the sea

Throughout history, new weapons have often made the difference between victory and defeat in war. During World War II, several nations introduced faster planes, large rockets, and radio-controlled bombs. And at the end of the war, the United States used the deadliest weapon ever invented—the atomic bomb.

V1 FLYING BOMBS

Germany's V1 flying bombs were powered by jet engines. They could fly about 400 miles (644 km) per hour. The V1 was nicknamed the "Buzz Bomb" because of the noise it made as it flew. It was used mostly to attack Great Britain, although some were also targeted at France and the Netherlands.

V2 ROCKET

Germany also built the first long-distance rocket. It could fly about 3,600 miles (5,794 km) per hour. It could deliver a 2,000-pound (907-kg) warhead. Some scientists who designed the V2 later worked on the U.S. program that sent rockets into space.

MESSERSCHMITT ME 262

In 1944 Germany began using the world's first fighter plane powered by a jet engine. The Messerschmitt ME 262 had a top speed of 540 miles (869 km) per hour. It flew about 100 miles (161 km) per hour faster than the best U.S. propeller planes. However, the ME 262 entered the war too late to have a major impact against the Allies.

THE ATOMIC BOMB

In 1945 the United States successfully created the first atomic bomb. In August of that year, the U.S. military dropped two atomic bombs on the Japanese cities of Hiroshima and Nagasaki. Japan surrendered soon afterward, bringing an end to World War II.

AFTER THE ATOMIC BOMB ·····················

A single atomic bomb equaled the explosive power of thousands of regular bombs. It also created a deadly form of energy called radiation. The atomic blasts in Japan, along with the resulting radiation, killed more than 300,000 people. The United States threatened to drop more atomic bombs on Japan. Facing total destruction, the Japanese government surrendered a few days after the second bomb blast.

GLOSSARY

ammunition (am-yuh-NI-shuhn)—bullets and other objects that can be fired from weapons

amphibious attack (am-FI-bee-uhs uh-TAK)—a military action involving forces landing and attacking from the sea

coalition (koh-uh-LISH-uhn)—an alliance of people, groups, or countries working together toward a common goal

infantry (IN-fuhn-tree)—a group of soldiers trained to fight and travel on foot

insignia (in-SIG-nee-uh)—a badge or design that shows someone's rank or membership in an organization

land mine (LAND MINE)—an explosive triggered by weight; land mines are usually hidden just under the surface of the ground

paratrooper (PAIR-uh-troop-ur)—a soldier trained to jump by parachute into battle

projectile (pruh-JEK-tuhl)—an object, such as a bullet or missile, that is thrown or shot through the air

radar (RAY-dar)—a device that uses radio waves to track the location of objects

READ MORE

Adams, Simon. *Eyewitness World War II.* DK Eyewitness Books. New York: DK Pub., 2007.

Chrisp, Peter. *World War II, Fighting for Freedom 1939–1945: The Story of the Conflict that Changed the World.* New York: Scholastic Reference, 2010.

Huey, Lois Miner. *Voices of World War II: Stories from the Front Lines.* Voices of War. Mankato, Minn.: Capstone Press, 2011.

Perritano, John. *World War II.* America at War. New York: Franklin Watts, 2010.

INTERNET SITES

FactHound offers a safe, fun way to find Internet sites related to this book. All of the sites on FactHound have been researched by our staff.

Here's all you do:

Visit *www.facthound.com*

Type in this code: 9781429676502

Super-cool stuff!

Check out projects, games and lots more at
www.capstonekids.com

INDEX